Polka Dot *Chr*

festive quilts with fun finishing edges

Sue Harvey • Sandy Boobar

Pine Tree Country Quilts

Polka Dot *Christmas*

by Sue Harvey and Sandy Boobar

Published by

All American Crafts, Inc.
7 Waterloo Road
Stanhope, NJ 07874
www.allamericancrafts.com

Publisher: **Jerry Cohen**

Chief Executive Officer: **Darren Cohen**

Product Development Director: **Brett Cohen**

Art Director: **Kelly Albertson**

Technical Illustrator: **Rory Byra**

Photography: **Van Zandbergen Photography**

Vice President/Quilting Advertising
  & Marketing: **Carol Newman**

Product Development Manager: **Pamela Mostek**

Every effort has been made to ensure that the information presented is accurate. Since we have no control over physical conditions, individual skills, or chosen tools and products, the publisher disclaims any liability for injuries, losses, untoward results, or any other damages which may result from the use of the information in this book. Thoroughly read the instructions for all products used to complete the projects in this book, paying particular attention to all cautions and warnings shown for that product to ensure their proper and safe use.

Printed in the China
©2010 All American Crafts, Inc
ISBN: 978-0-9819762-3-5
Library of Congress Control Number: 2010923345

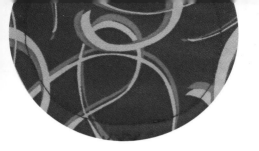

Special Thanks to:

Our families for putting up with a crazy couple of months of
planning, stitching, and flying pieces of polka dots

Carol Newman for thinking of us when All American Crafts decided to
publish a book of Christmas designs and for her hours agonizing over photographing the projects

Connie Newhall for hand-stitching all those never-ending bindings and the
much-appreciated (and much-needed) advice and help on the many "sewing" projects

Melany Thurlow for the marathon weekend of piecing

Pamela Mostek, for her guidance in narrowing the focus of this
book and her suggestions for taking some of the designs from so-so to WOW

The following companies for providing materials, fabrics, tools, and supplies
for many of the projects: Robert Kaufman Fabrics, Michael Miller Fabrics,
Benartex, May Arts Ribbon, EZ Quilting, Fairfield Processing, and Coats & Clark

Ethan Allen Furniture in Dickson City, Pennsylvania, for use of the store for photography

And Offray Ribbon for supplying the polka-dot ribbons for the photography

Sue Harvey and *Sandy Boobar*

Contents

Dotty & Edgy   What a Combination!

We know that we've been called "dotty" for a long time, but are we thought of as "edgy"? If it means on the cutting edge or avant-garde, perhaps not. But if it means using lots of polka dots in our quilts and doing something a little extra to the edges, then you will soon find out how fitting that is!

We love polka dots—everything from bright, bouncy circles on a crisp white background to subtle, muted dots on warm backgrounds. Regardless of color, style, or size, polka dots always seem to say "Happy!" when used in a quilt. They have been around for more than 150 years, fading into the background in some years and springing back into popularity in others. Today, many fabric collections contain a polka-dot coordinate giving us almost endless choices to add to our quilts.

Now, how does the edgy description fit? We've always tried to take our designs a step farther by doing something unique with a border or adding something dimensional. We love prairie points for fun and playful quilts like those for little boys and half-circles for soft, cute quilts for little girls.

We often include folded strips in our bindings to add just a touch of interest. We've used frayed chenille for edgings, and once we even added a fringe that we designed and knitted ourselves (thank you, Sandy's mom, for the quick knitting lessons). If all this doesn't mean edgy, it definitely means dotty!

In this book, we've combined polka dots and edges in a variety of designs to make for the holidays. Lots of these designs are in nontraditional colors—pink and green, lime green and red, robin's-egg blue and rust. Each one started with a polka dot. We let the dots take us where they wanted, and we love the results.

Decorate your table with one of our five toppers and runners. *Holiday Maze* is a bit more traditional than the rest with its creamy background and prairie points. We used dimensional circles to decorate the ends of *Merry Christmas Table Runner*. The bright red and grassy green of *Woven Wreaths* sparkle against its white background and the candy-stripe binding brings to mind bowls of ribbon candy that come out at this special time of year. Make a quick *Ornament Wreath* topper with single scallop borders to set off a beautiful poinsettia or bowl of shiny ornaments or stitch one for a last-minute gift. Show your fun side with our *Wonky Northern Lights* runner. There's nothing to match, nothing to worry about fitting in its unique style of piecing.

Enjoy the warmth and family time of the season while surrounded by cheerful throws and quilts for your favorite chair or sofa. *Poinsettia Hopscotch* is so easy to piece and a cinch to finish with its folded strip binding. The girly girl in your family is sure to adore the pink, red and lime-green color scheme and the ruffle and bow embellishments of the *Ornament Dance* quilt. Our *Dots & Curves* quilt will add a subtle touch of Christmas to a bed, daybed, or futon.

Stitch up a tree full of *Gift-It Totes* and forget about buying paper and bows. Or make them to replace birthday, Mother's Day, Father's Day, baby shower, anniversary, and wedding gift bags. Fill one with flowers to welcome a new neighbor or with comfort items to visit a sick friend.

Actually, with the exception of our *Waiting for Santa Stocking,* all of the projects in this book can easily be used anytime of the year. Of course, if you do come up with a way to leave a stocking hanging on your mantel all year without your friends deciding that you have gone beyond edgy to the brink of dotty, let us know your secret!

Enjoy the book,

Sue and Sandy

The Finishing Edges

Nothing gives your quilt more zing than an eye-catching finish.
Rather than just straight edges, try scallops of all sizes and shapes, prairie points with a difference, raw-edged bindings, or, for a super-edgy finish, our polka-dot finishing edge.
In this section you'll find instructions for each type of finish.
Refer back to it as you complete the projects.

Scalloped Finishing Edge

Add the scalloped-edge finish after you complete the quilting in order to stabilize the quilt and prevent stretching when you cut the scallops. Prepare the full-size scallop pattern on page 24 and cut a template from template plastic or heavy cardboard. Because of differences in stitching and quilting, the completed size of each quilt may vary. To make the scallop pattern fit the sides of your quilt, make adjustments in the scallops as we explain in the following steps.

1. Begin tracing the scallop pattern onto the quilt border as noted in the instructions for the project. Continue tracing around the template until you complete the scallops on each side.

2. The scallops should either meet at the center of the quilt side or one scallop should be centered at the center of the side. You may need to elongate or shorten the center scallops to make them fit.

For example, in *Dots & Curves*, we marked two scallops from the corner toward the center. Then we realized we had too much room for just one more scallop before the center of the side, but not enough room for two. We marked the center of the border with a pin, then we put the template at the end of the marked scallops, marked the scallop from the inside corner to the outside edge and stopped. We moved the template along the border so the other end was at the pin and marked from the outside edge to the inside corner at the pin.

We marked two more scallops and an elongated scallop at the other end of the border to make two elongated scallops—one on either side of the center pin. We repeated this on the other side of the quilt to make two longer scallops in the center of each side edge.

3. To mark a corner scallop, place the template at the end of the last scallop previously traced on the border. Mark from the inside corner of the template where it aligns with the end of the last scallop to the outside edge of the border. You will be marking half the scallop shape. Repeat on the end of the last scallop on the

adjacent side of the corner, again marking only half of the scallop. This will create a pointed corner for your scalloped border. Repeat to mark scallops at each corner of the quilt.

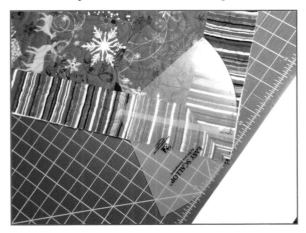

4. Using sharp scissors or small rotary cutter, cut around the marked curves. Refer to Adding the Binding on page 93 to prepare bias biding.

5. Begin stitching the binding to the quilt on the outside edge of a scallop, leaving a tail unstitched. Be careful not to pull and stretch the binding as you stitch; let it ease along the curve. Stop stitching at the inside corner point, leaving the needle in the fabric.

6. Raise the presser foot, pivot the quilt, and arrange the binding along the edge of the next scallop.

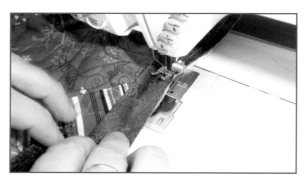

7. Stitch around the scallop to the next inside point and repeat the previous steps. Repeat to sew binding to the entire edge of the quilt. Join the ends, referring to Adding the Binding on page 93.

Tip

Our favorite tool for marking quilt borders is the Easy Scallop™ template by Darlene Zimmerman from EZ Quilting.

8. Turn binding to the back of the quilt and pin in place, forming a small tuck at each inside point on both sides of the quilt. Hand-stitch the binding in place to finish the quilt.

Prairie Points Finishing Edge

Prairie points are folded squares or rectangles of fabrics that add a fun, zigzag edging to a quilt. They can be larger or smaller than those we added to the edges of our quilts. They can also overlap or be positioned so they come together with no overlap. You can even alternate larger and smaller prairie points as we did in *Holiday Maze* on page 80 for a more irregular finishing edge. Refer to the project instructions for the number and size of the fabric pieces needed for the prairie points for each project and refer to the following instructions.

1. Layer the quilt top, batting, and backing, and quilt your quilt. Stop stitching approximately 1" from the edge on all sides.

2. Fold a fabric square in half diagonally and press (see project instructions for size of square). Fold in half diagonally again and press to complete one prairie point. Repeat to make the number of prairie points needed for the project.

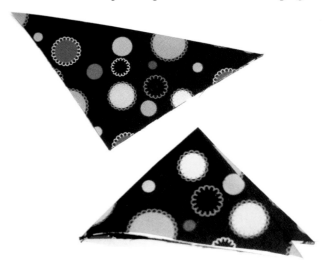

3. Fold the backing away from the quilt edges. Trim the batting even with the quilt top, then unfold the backing and trim it to ¼" beyond the edge of the batting and quilt top.

4. Fold the backing away from the quilt edges again and pin to hold.

5. Evenly space prairie points along one edge of the quilt with raw edges aligned (see project instructions for number of prairie points needed per side and specific spacing information). Pin in place. Repeat to evenly space and pin prairie points along each side of the quilt. **Note:** If another size of prairie points is used in the project, place them between the pinned prairie points and pin in place.

6. Machine-baste the points in place near the edge of the quilt, then stitch ¼" from the edge through all layers.

7. Press the prairie points upright along the edge of the quilt and the seam allowance to the back of the quilt.

8. Unfold the backing and turn the edges under to meet the stitching line on the prairie points. Pin. Hand-stitch the backing to the back of the prairie points.

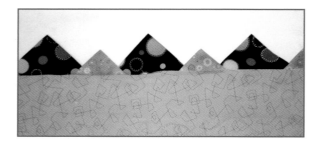

Double-Frayed Finishing Edge

For a new twist to binding, try the double-frayed version. Add it to your quilt after the quilting is completed, just like traditional bindings. Refer to the project instructions for the length, width, and number of strips needed for that project.

1. Fold the binding strips in half lengthwise and press.

2. Draw a line ¼" from the outside edge on the back of the quilt.

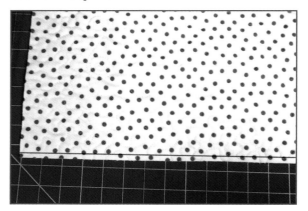

3. Place the folded edge of a binding strip along the ¼" line on one side and pin in place. Repeat on the opposite side.

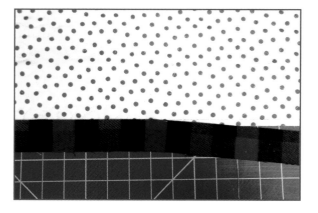

4. Stitch close to the folded edge of the binding strips. Trim the ends of the strips even with the edges of the quilt.

5. Bring the raw edges of the binding strips to the front of the quilt. Pin in place.

6. On the quilt front, stitch the binding ¼" from the edge of the quilt.

7. Pin binding strips to the remaining sides along the ¼" line on the top and bottom of the quilt back. Trim the binding strips ¼" beyond the quilt edge at each end.

8. Unfold the ends of the strips and turn under ¼" under. Press.

9. Refold the ends and pin to the back of the quilt, making sure the ends align with the side edges of the quilt. Stitch on the back and the front in the same manner as the previous sides. Stitch close to the edge at the end of each strip to hold in place.

10. With sharp scissors, cut close to the stitching line every ¼" to ½" along the length of each binding strip to fringe the edges.

11. Remove the cross threads of the fringe to fray. Use a stiff-bristle brush to remove additional threads and to fluff the fringe.

Tip

When you are finished fraying the binding, give the quilt a good shake outside and then use a lint roller to pick up any stray threads.

Binding Insert Finishing Edge

Whether it's ruffled or flat against the quilt, adding another layer to your bindings will definitely give your quilt an edge. Add this great finish after the quilting is completed. Refer to each project for the specific lengths needed for the binding insert.

Ruffled Insert

1. Cut four strips of 1½"-wide ribbon according to the lengths needed for the project. Sew a line of gathering stitches ⅛" from one edge of the ribbon and another line ¼" from the edge.

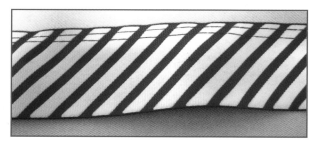

2. Lightly gather the strips until they are the lengths given in the project instructions. Machine-baste to hold the gathers in place.

3. Place and pin the ribbons along opposite sides of the quilt with the gathered edge of the ribbon aligned with the raw edges of the quilt. Machine-stitch in place. Repeat to add ribbons to the remaining sides.

4. Bind the quilt, using binding strips cut ¾" wider than usual to allow for the extra bulk.

Flat Insert

1. Sew the insert strips for the project together into one long strip. Cut the strips to the lengths given for the project.

2. Fold the strips in half lengthwise and press. Place a strip along the outer edge of one side of the quilt with raw edges aligned and the folded edge of the strip towards the quilt center. Pin in place. Repeat on each edge of the quilt. Machine-baste in place.

3. Bind the quilt, using binding strips cut ¼" wider than usual to allow for the extra bulk.

Polka-Dot Finishing Edge

For a super-dramatic finish to your quilt, add these super-sized polka dots! Refer to the project instructions for the number of polka dots you'll need, and trace the polka-dot pattern on page 36 for the template. Trace around it onto template plastic or lightweight cardboard.

1. Using the polka-dot template, mark the number of 4" circles you'll need for your project onto the wrong side of the fabric designated for the polka dots. Leave ½" between the polka dots.

2. With right sides together, place the fabric marked with polka dots onto the backing fabric. Place the batting piece listed in the instructions on the bottom. Pin the layers to hold them together.

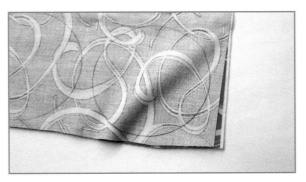

3. Stitch on each marked circle, leaving a 3" opening for turning.

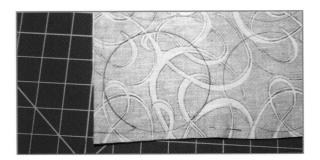

4. Cut around each circle, ¼" from the stitching line. Turn the circle right side out through the opening, and turn the seam allowance of the opening to the inside. Press. Hand-stitch the opening closed. Stitch ¼" inside the edge of each polka dot with matching thread.

5. Arrange the polka dots as directed in the project instructions. Mark the position of each with a pin in the quilt.

6. Butt a polka dot against the quilt edge at one of the pins. Stitch the polka dots to the quilt edge using a stitch that moves side to side, such as a wide zigzag stitch, to catch both the polka dot and the quilt. Stitch along the butted edge just enough to hold the circle in place. Repeat to add a polka dot at each pin. Add a polka dot at each corner, if needed.

Tip

To make stitching easier when you're making a large number of polka dots, cut the large traced piece into sections with four circles or less in each section.

Polka-Dot Quilts .... and More!

Dots & Curves

Sometimes we find a collection of fabrics that we just don't want to split up.
We love the large circles and polka dots in this quilt combined with the birds and reindeer in the border and block fabric. Dig out that holiday collection that you've been waiting to use. We bet it will work as well in this curvy design as our fabrics do.

Finished Size: 80" x 94"
Finished Block Size: 15" x 18½"
Skill Level: Confident Beginner

Fabric & Stuff

Yardage is based on 42"-wide cotton fabric.

- 2½ yards green holiday print
- 1¾ yards cream polka dot
- 1⅓ yards light green print
- 1⅛ yards red print
- 1⅛ yards stripe
- 1 yard green tonal
- ¾ yard cream snowflake print
- 88" x 102" backing piece
- 88" x 102" batting piece
- Threads to match fabrics
- 12" scallop template or template material
- Chalk pencil or other marking tool

Cutting the Pieces

From the green holiday print, cut
Two 5½" x 78½" strips cut along the length of the fabric
Five 5½" x 31" strips, cut across the remaining width of the fabric
Four 8½" x 31" strips, then cut into sixteen 6" x 8½" rectangles

From the cream polka dot, cut
Two 13½" x 42" strips
Two 15" x 42" strips, then cut into thirty-two 2½" x 15" strips

From the light green print, cut
Two 9½" x 42" strips
Two 12" x 42" strips, then cut into thirty-two 2½" x 12" strips

From the red print, cut
Two 2" x 42" strips
Four 2½" x 42" strips
Seven 2½" x 42" strips

From the stripe, cut
Nine 3½" x 42" strips

From the green tonal, cut
2½"-wide bias strips to total 430" for binding

From the cream snowflake print, cut
Two 6" x 42" strips
One 8½" x 42" strip, then cut into sixteen 2" x 8½" strips

Making the Blocks

1. Sew a 2" x 42" red strip lengthwise to a 6" x 42" cream snowflake strip. Press seam toward the red strip. Repeat to make a second strip set. Cut the strip sets into thirty-two 2¼" A segments.

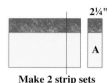

Make 2 strip sets

2. Sew a 2½" x 42" red strip lengthwise to a 9½" x 42" light green strip. Press seam toward the red strip. Repeat to make a second strip set. Cut the strip sets into thirty-two 2" B segments.

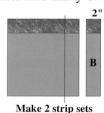

Make 2 strip sets

3. Sew a 2½" x 42" red strip lengthwise to a 13½" x 42" cream polka-dot strip. Press seam toward the red strip. Repeat to make a second strip set. Cut the strip sets into thirty-two 2½" C segments.

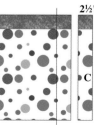

Make 2 strip sets

4. Sew a 2" x 8½" cream snowflake strip to the left side of eight 6" x 8½" green holiday rectangles and to the right side of the remaining eight rectangles. Press seams toward the cream strips. **Note:** Press all seams toward each new strip and segment added in the following steps.

Make 8   Make 8

5. Sew an A segment from step 1 to the top and bottom of each unit from step 4 as shown.

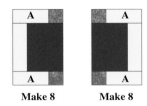

Make 8   Make 8

6. Sew a 2½" x 12" light green strip to opposite long sides of each pieced unit. Sew a B segment from step 2 to the top and bottom.

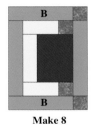 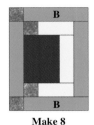

Make 8   Make 8

7. Sew a 2½" x 15" cream polka-dot strip to opposite long sides of each pieced unit and a C segment from step 3 to the top and bottom to complete eight 15½" x 19" A blocks and eight 15½" x 19" B blocks.

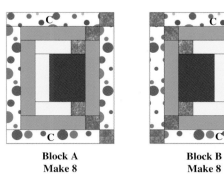

Block A
Make 8

Block B
Make 8

Putting It Together

1. Join four of A blocks to make an A row. Repeat to make a second A row. Press seams toward the left.

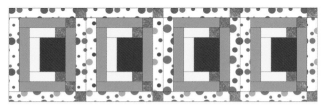

Make 2

2. Join four B blocks to make a B row. Repeat to make a second B row. Press seams toward the right.

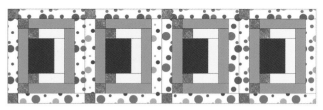

Make 2

3. Beginning with an A row, join the rows alternately to complete the 60½" x 74½" quilt center. Press.

4. Sew the remaining 2½" x 42" red strips short ends together to make one long strip. Press. Cut two 74½" strips and two 64½" strips. Sew the longer strips to the long sides of the quilt center and the shorter strips to the top and bottom. Press.

5. Sew the 5½" x 78½" green holiday print strips to the long sides of the quilt center. Sew the 5½" x 31" green holiday strips together to make one long strip. Cut two 74½"strips. Sew the strips to the top and bottom of the quilt.

6. Sew the 3½" x 42" stripe strips together to make one long strip. Cut two 98" strips and two 84" strips. Refer to Mitered Borders on page 92 to add borders to the quilt.

7. Referring to Layering, Basting and Quilting on page 93, finish the quilt top. Trim the batting and backing even with the quilt top.

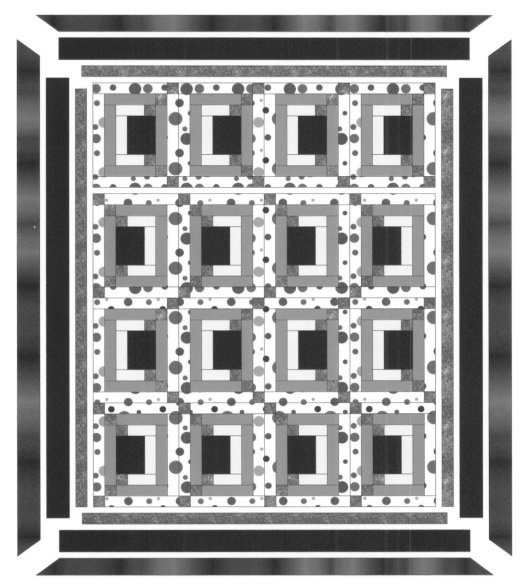

Quilt Layout

Adding the Scalloped Finishing Edge

To prepare your quilt for scalloped edges, measure 5" on both sides of each corner and mark with pins. Place a pin at the center of each side. Referring to Scalloped Finishing Edge on page 8, begin tracing the scallops at the 5" pins and complete the scalloped edges. Add bias binding to the edges to complete the quilt.

Scalloped Finishing Edge

Scallop Pattern
Enlarge 155%

Oh! Christmas Tree

Stop looking for the perfect Christmas tree! Who needs it?
This lopsided, haphazard little tree says Merry Christmas just like its
well-groomed cousins. The double-frayed binding adds a warm and cozy
finish that entices everyone to give it a quick touch.

Finished Size: 21" x 30"
Skill Level: Beginner

Fabric & Stuff

Yardage is based on 42"-wide cotton fabric

- ¾ yard cream/green polka dot
- ½ yard lime-green tonal
- ½ yard woven plaid
- ⅛ yard each of three different bright tonals
- Scrap of gold fabric for the star

- 29" x 38" backing piece
- 29" x 38" batting piece
- Thread to match fabrics
- Chalk pencil or other marking tool
- Stiff-bristle brush
- Assorted bright buttons
- Assorted bright colors of embroidery floss

Cutting the Pieces

From the cream/green polka dot, cut
One 12½" x 21½" piece
Two 3" x 25½" strips
Two 3" x 21½" strips

From the lime-green tonal, cut
One 2½" x 42" strip, then cut into
assorted pieces, 2" to 4" long

From the woven plaid, cut
Two 3" x 32" strips for binding
Two 3" x 23" strips for binding

From each of the three bright tonals, cut
One 2½" x 42" strip, then cut into
assorted pieces, 2" to 4" long

Making the Tree Center

1. Cut two 10" x 12" strips of fusible web. Referring to the manufacturer's instructions, fuse to the wrong side of the remaining lime-green tonal.

2. From the fused fabric, cut one 9" x 9" square, one 7" x 7" square, and one 5" x 5" square.

3. Cut each square twice diagonally, but not from corner to corner. Place your ruler below the corner on one side and above the corner on the opposite side and cut. Then repeat this with the remaining corners.

4. Arrange two pieces from each square on the 12½" x 21½" cream/green polka-dot piece, beginning about 1" above the bottom edge and leaving at least 3" above the top piece. Tilt the pieces in different directions as desired.

5. Remove the paper backing from each piece and fuse the tree in place.

6. Trace the star pattern on page 30 onto the paper side of the remaining fusible web. Cut out leaving a margin around the traced shape.

7. Fuse the shape onto the wrong side of the gold scrap and cut out the star on the traced lines. Remove the paper backing. Fuse to the top of the tree.

8. Using a buttonhole stitch and thread to match the fabrics, stitch around the tree and star pieces.

Putting It Together

1. Randomly sew the bright color and lime-green pieces together on the 2½" edges to make a long strip. Press seams in one direction. Cut two 21½" strips and two 16½" strips. Sew the longer strips to the long sides of the tree center and the shorter strips to the top and bottom. Press seams toward the tree center.

2. Sew the 3" x 25½" cream/green polka-dot strips to the long sides and the 3" x 21½" strips to the top and bottom to complete the top. Press seams toward the strips.

Tip

Don't throw the leftover pieces away.
Use them to make a second quilt to give as a gift.

Finishing the Quilt

1. Referring to Layering, Basting, and Quilting on page 93, finish the quilt top.

2. Using the two 3" x 23" and two 3" x 32" woven plaid strips, refer to Double-Frayed Finishing Edge on page 12 to add the frayed binding to the quilt.

3. Tie buttons to the tree with two or three strands of embroidery floss.

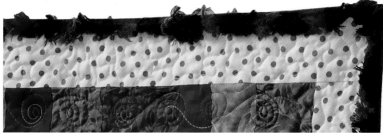

Double-Frayed Finishing Edge

Try It Again

Just think of the ways this simple little tree could be used. Make a tiny version to fuse on paper for your holiday cards. Add one to the front of a *Waiting for Santa Stocking*. Or, do as we did, and use it to decorate a *Gift-It Tote* on page 62.

Star Pattern

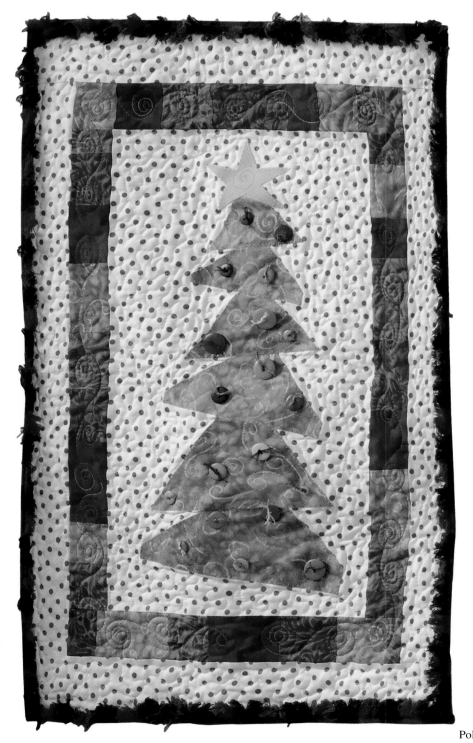

Ornament Dance

We started this quilt with a contemporary tree print and
ended with a girly Christmas quilt that will make every little princess happy!

Finished Size: 54" x 66"
Skill Level: Beginner

Fabric & Stuff

Yardage is based on 42"-wide cotton fabric

- 1⅞ yards red mottled
- 1⅔ yards tree print
- 1 yard light green solid
- ⅜ yard red polka dot
- 62" x 74" backing piece
- 62" x 74" batting piece
- Thread to match fabrics
- ¾ yard 18"-wide fusible web
- Template plastic
- 7 yards ½"-wide, red and white diagonal stripe ribbon
- 10 yards 1½"-wide, red and white diagonal stripe ribbon
- Fray Check or other fray preventative

Cutting the Pieces

From the red mottled, cut
Five 3½" x 42" strips, then cut into
sixty 3½" x 3½" squares
Eleven 2½" x 42" strips
Six 3" x 42" strips for binding

From the tree print, cut
Two 4" x 55½" strips cut along the length
of the fabric
Three 4" x 34" strips cut across the remaining
width of the fabric
Six 6½" x 34" strips cut across the remaining
width of the fabric, then cut into
thirty 6½" x 6½" squares

From the light green solid, cut
Three 6½" x 42" strips, then cut into
eighteen 6½" x 6½" squares
Five 2" x 42" strips

Making the Quilt Center

1. Mark a diagonal line on the wrong side of each
3½" x 3½" red square. With right sides together,
place a marked red square on a corner of each
6½" x 6½" tree print square. Stitch on the
marked line. Trim the seam allowance to ¼"
and press the red triangle toward the corner.

2. Repeat on the opposite corner of the square to
make a total of 30 blocks.

Tip: Using Directional Fabric

If your fabric is directional as ours was,
you'll need to make 18 of the units from
steps 1 and 2, then reverse the corners of
the triangles to make 12 reversed units.

3. Trace the polka-dot pattern on page 36 onto
template plastic and cut out the polka-dot
template.

4. Cut two 9" x 21" strips of fusible web. Fuse
to the wrong side of the red polka-dot fabric,
following the manufacturer's instructions.
Using the polka-dot template, trace eighteen
polka dots onto the paper side of the fabric.
Cut out the polka dots on the marked lines.
Remove the paper backing.

5. Fuse a polka dot to each 6½" x 6½" light green square, 1" from the bottom edge and 1¼" from each side edge.

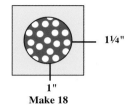

1¼"

1"
Make 18

6. Using matching thread, machine buttonhole stitch around each fused polka dot to complete the ornament units.

Putting It Together

1. Arrange and sew tree and ornament units together into eight rows as shown. Press seams in rows in opposite directions. Join the rows to complete the 36½" x 48½" quilt center.

2. Sew the 2" x 42" light green strips together into one long strip. Cut two 48½" and two 39½" strips. Sew the longer strips to the sides and the shorter strips to the top and bottom. Press seams toward the strips.

3. Sew five 2½" x 42" red strips together into one long strip. Cut two 51½" strips and two 43½" strips. Sew the longer strips to opposite long sides of the quilt center and the shorter strips to the top and bottom. Press.

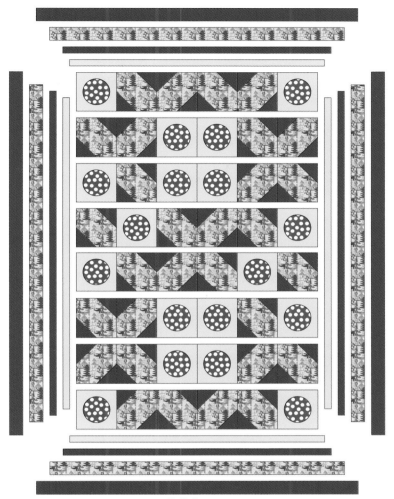

Quilt Layout

4. Sew the 4" x 55½" tree print strips to the long sides of the quilt center. Sew the 4" x 34" tree print strips together to make one long strip. Cut two 50½" strips. Sew these strips to the top and bottom. Press.

5. Sew the remaining six 2½" x 42" red strips together into one long strip. Cut two 62½" strips and two 54½" strips. Sew the longer strips to the sides and the shorter strips to the top and bottom. Press.

6. Referring to Layering, Basting, and Quilting on page 93, complete the quilt center.

Adding the finishing Touches

1. Cut eighteen 14" pieces of ½"-wide stripe ribbon. Make bows and stitch to the top of each polka-dot circle. To avoid hard knots, form two loops with tails and stitch between the loops to secure them to the quilt. Cut the ends at an angle and apply fray preventative.

2. Cut two 97" pieces and two 83" pieces of 1½"-wide stripe ribbon. Gather the longer strips to 66½" and the shorter strips to 54½". Add to the quilt referring to Ruffled Insert on page 14.

3. Referring to Adding the Binding on page 93, use the 3" x 42" red strips and bind the edges.

Ruffled Binding Insert

More Polka Dots

Spread the polka-dot ornaments around to other holiday projects like the *Gift-It Tote*. Instead of a ribbon bow, we cut a fabric strip 3" x 14", pressed the edges into the center, folded it in half and stitched along the long edges. Then we made loops and attached it to the top of the ornament with a button. Quick, easy and sure to be appreciated.

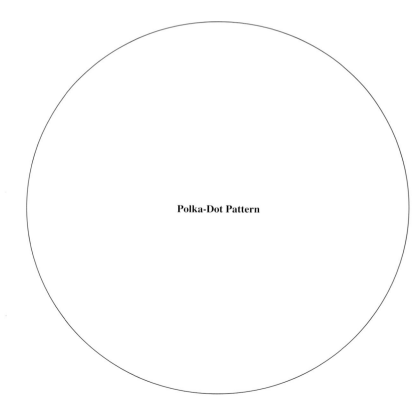

Polka-Dot Pattern

Polka-Dot Tree Skirt

We were challenged to make a project using fabrics that were all medium shades. So, we gathered a bunch of green and red prints and mixed them up in a pieced block—and of course, we added the green polka dots to separate them a bit. To continue the theme, we decided to add polka dots to the outside edge. We love the fresh look it gave to the edge of the tree skirt.

Finished Size: 48½" x 48½", including polka-dot edge
Finished Block Size: 12½" x 12½"
Skill Level: Intermediate

Fabric & Stuff

Yardage is based on 42"-wide cotton fabric

- 2 yards red swirl print
- ⅝ yard green and red print
- ¾ yard green print 1
- ⅝ yard of green print 2
- ¼ yard green print 3
- ⅓ yard green polka dot
- 48" x 48" backing piece
- 48" x 48" batting piece for quilt
- 21" x 36" batting piece for polka-dot edges
- Thread to match fabrics
- 6" to 8" circle template for tree-skirt center

Cutting the Pieces

From the red swirl print, cut
One 2" x 42" strip, then cut into
four 2" x 2" squares
One 36" x 42" strip, then cut into
two 21" x 36" pieces
2½"-wide bias strips totaling 240"
for binding

From the green and red flower print, cut
Two 7½" x 42" strips, then cut into
thirty-six 2¼" x 7½" rectangles

From the green print 1, cut
One 3¾" x 42" strip, then cut into
nine 3¾" x 3¾" squares, cut twice
diagonally to make thirty-six of triangle A
Five 3⅜" x 42" strips, then cut into
fifty-four 3⅜" x 3⅜" squares, cut
once diagonally to make one hundred
eight of triangle B

From the green print 2, cut
Four 2¾" x 42" strips
Two 3⅜" x 42" strips, then cut into
eighteen 3⅜" x 3⅜" squares, cut once
diagonally to make thirty-six of triangle C

From the green print 3, cut
Two 3" x 42" strips

From the green polka dot, cut
Four 2" x 42" strips, then cut into
twelve 2" x 13" sashing strips

Tip: Keep Them Straight!

When you're sewing with a number of pieces that are close to the same size and shape, such as the triangles in this project, use plastic sandwich bags to keep them sorted. Put all of the A triangles in one bag and label the outside with a marking pen. Repeat with bags for triangles B and C.

Making the Blocks

1. Sew a 3" x 42" strip of green print 3 lengthwise between two 2¾" x 42" strips of green print 2. Press seams toward green print 3. Repeat to make two strip sets total. Cut the strip sets into nine 7½" center units.

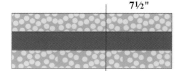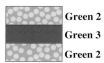

Green 2
Green 3
Green 2

7½"

Make 2 strip sets

2. Sew a green B triangle to a green C triangle. Press seam toward the B triangles. Sew a green B triangle to each side of the C triangle as shown. Press seams toward the B triangles. Sew a 2¼" x 7½" green and red print rectangle to the long side. Press seam toward the rectangle. Repeat to make a total of thirty-six units.

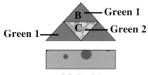

Green 1 — B — Green 1
Green 1 — C — Green 2

Make 36

3. Sew a triangle unit to opposite ends of each center unit. Press seams toward the center units.

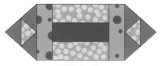

Make 9

4. Sew a green A triangle to each end of the rectangle in each of the remaining units from step 2 as shown. Press seams toward A.

5. Sew a unit from step 4 to the remaining sides of the center unit to complete nine 13" x 13" blocks. Press seams toward the triangle units.

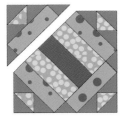 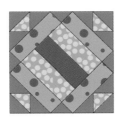

Putting It Together

1. Sew two green polka-dot sashing strips between three blocks to make one row. Press seams toward the sashing strips. Repeat to make three rows total.

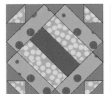 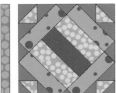 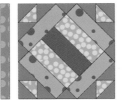

Make 3

2. Sew two 2" red swirl squares between three sashing strips. Press seams toward the sashing strips. Repeat to make two sashing rows total.

Make 2

3. Join the block rows alternately with the sashing rows to complete the pieced top. Press.

4. Referring to Layering, Basting, and Quilting on page 93, complete the quilt top.

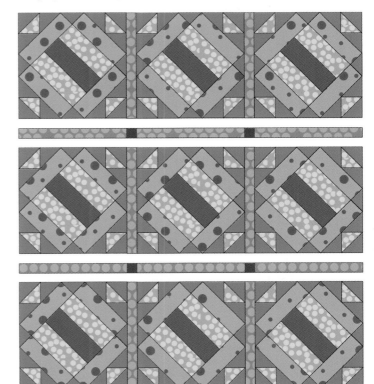

5. Using the 6" to 8" circle template, trace a circle in the center block. Cut a straight line from the circle to the midpoint of one outside edge. Cut out the center circle to complete the opening for the tree skirt.

6. Referring to Adding the Binding on page 93, prepare bias binding and bind the outside and inside edges.

Adding the Polka-Dot Finishing Edge

Referring to Polka-Dot Finishing Edge on page 14 for instructions on completing the polka dots, trace twenty-eight polka dots onto one of the 21" x 36" red swirl print pieces. After completing the polka dots, position and sew one at each corner and six on each side of the tree skirt.

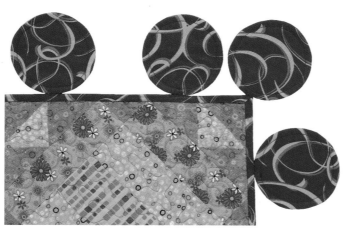

Polka-Dot Finishing Edge

A Matched Set

For a total holiday look, use the same fabrics that you used in the tree skirt to make the *Merry Christmas Table Runner* on page 68. Place it on a coffee table or sofa table for added polka-dot pizzazz!

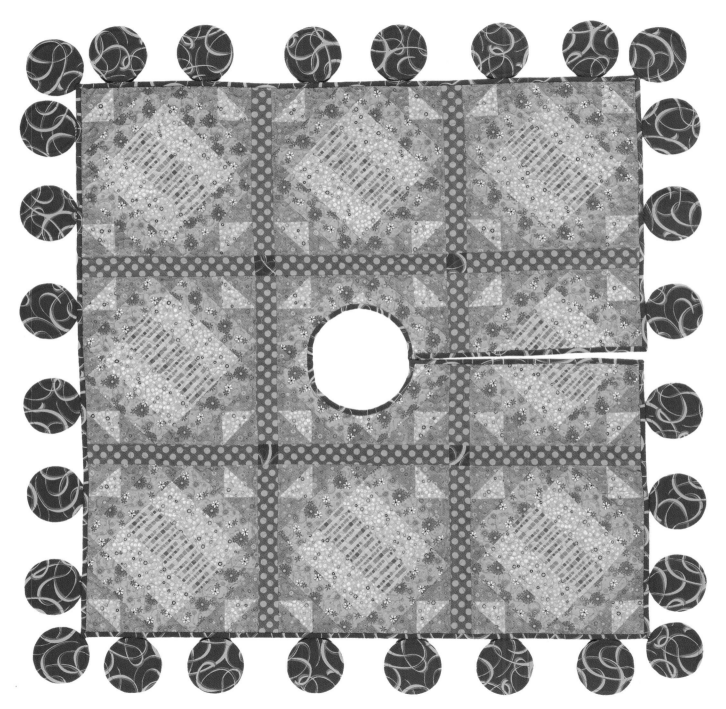

Woven Wreaths

Happy! Fun! Lively! The red and green polka dots just seem to dance on their crisp white background. Put this quilt on your table with a big bowl of red and green Christmas balls or throw it over the back of a sofa. It's an easy way to wish all your visitors a Merry Christmas.

Finished Size: 58" x 58"
Skill Level: Intermediate

Fabric & Stuff

Yardage is based on 42"-wide cotton fabric

- 2 yards white, red, and green polka dot
- 1½ yards green tonal
- 1½ yards red tonal
- 66" x 66" backing piece
- 66" x 66" batting piece
- Thread to match fabrics
- Template plastic

Cutting the Pieces

From the white, red, and green polka dot, cut
Two 6½" x 42" strips, then cut into twelve 6½" x 6½" squares
Four 2⅞" x 42" strips, then cut into forty-four 2⅞" x 2⅞" squares, cut four squares once diagonally to make eight triangles
One 4⅞" x 42" strip, then cut into two 4⅞" squares, cut once diagonally to make four triangles
One 2½" x 42" strip, then cut one into one 2½" x 10½" strip and two 2½" x 4½" strips
One 4½" x 42" strip, then cut into four 4½" x 10½" strips
Six 2½" x 42" strips

From the green tonal, cut
Six 2½" x 42" strips
One 4½" x 42" strip, then cut into four 4½" x 4½" squares and two 2½" x 2½" squares
Four 2¼" x 42" strips, then cut into ten 2¼" x 14" strips for binding

From the red tonal, cut
Six 2½" x 42" strips
Three 4⅞" x 42" strips, then cut into twenty 4⅞" x 4⅞" squares
One 4½" x 42" strip, then cut into four 4½" x 4½" squares and two 2½" x 2½" squares
Four 2¼" x 42" strips, then cut into ten 2¼" x 14" strips for binding

Making the Blocks

1. Sew a 2½" x 42" polka-dot strip lengthwise between a 2½" x 42" green strip and a 2½" x 42" red strip. Press seams away from the center strip. Repeat to make a total of six strip sets. Cut the strip sets into thirty-six 6½" stripe segments.

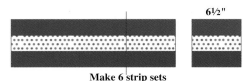

Make 6 strip sets

2. Mark a diagonal line on the wrong side of each 2⅞" x 2⅞" white polka-dot square. Place a square on one corner of a 4⅞" x 4⅞" red square. Stitch on the marked line, trim seam allowance to ¼", and press toward the corners. Repeat on the opposite corner of the red square. Repeat to make a total of 20 units.

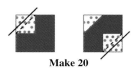

Make 20

3. Cut each unit in half diagonally through the white corners to make forty triangles.

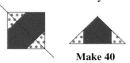

Make 40

4. Prepare a template for the Woven Wreaths A Pattern given on page 95. Cut 22 A pieces from green tonal and two A pieces from red tonal.

To stabilize the angled bias edges of the A pieces, apply
spray starch after cutting them out and press dry.

5. Sew a pieced triangle unit from step 3 to opposite sides of twenty green A pieces to complete the X units. Press seams toward the A pieces.

Make 20

6. Sew a small polka-dot triangle to two sides of two 2½" red squares and two 2½" green squares. Press seams toward the polka-dot triangles.

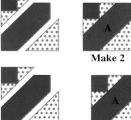

Make 2   **Make 2**

7. Sew a green A piece to the red units and a red A piece to the green units. Press seams toward the A pieces. Sew a large polka-dot triangle to the remaining A side of each unit to make four corner units. Press seams toward the A pieces.

Make 2

Make 2

8. Sew a 2½" x 4½" polka-dot strip between a 4½" red square and a 4½" green square. Press seams toward the squares. Repeat to make two pieced units. Sew a 2½" x 10½" polka-dot strip between the two pieced units and add a 4½" x 10½" polka-dot strip to opposite sides. Press seams toward the pieced units.

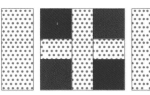

Make 2

9. Sew a 4½" x 10½" polka-dot piece between a 4½" red square and a 4½" green square. Press seams toward the squares. Repeat to make two strips total. Sew a strip to the top and bottom to complete the center unit. Press seams toward the strips.

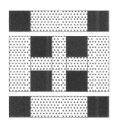

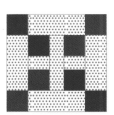

Putting It Together

1. Select 10 stripe segments, four X units, the center unit and four 6½" white squares. Arrange and join the units and squares to make the center row. Press all seams toward the stripe segments.

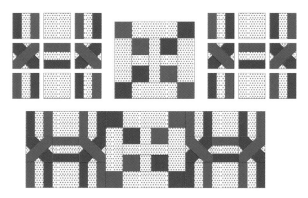

2. Select 13 stripe segments, eight X units, one each red and green corner units and four 6½" white squares. Arrange and join the units and squares to make the top row. Press all seams toward the stripe segments. Repeat to make the bottom row.

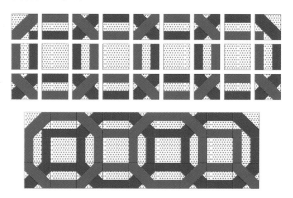

3. Sew the center row between the top and bottom rows, to complete the 54½" x 54½" quilt center. Press seams toward the center row.

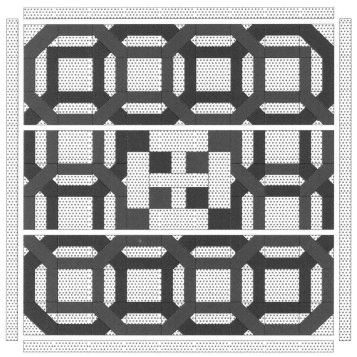

Quilt Layout

4. Sew the 2½" x 42" polka-dot strips together to make one long strip. Press. Cut two 54½" strips and two 58½" strips. Sew the shorter strips to opposite sides of the quilt center and the longer strips to the remaining sides to complete the quilt top. Press seams toward the strips.

5. Referring to Layering, Basting, and Quilting on page 93, complete the quilt top.

Adding the Candy Stripe Binding

Join the red and green 2½" x 14" binding strips with diagonal seams, alternating colors. Press the seams to one side. Refer to Adding the Binding on page 93 to add the candy stripe binding to finish the quilt.

Template for this quilt given on page 95.

Candy Stripe Binding

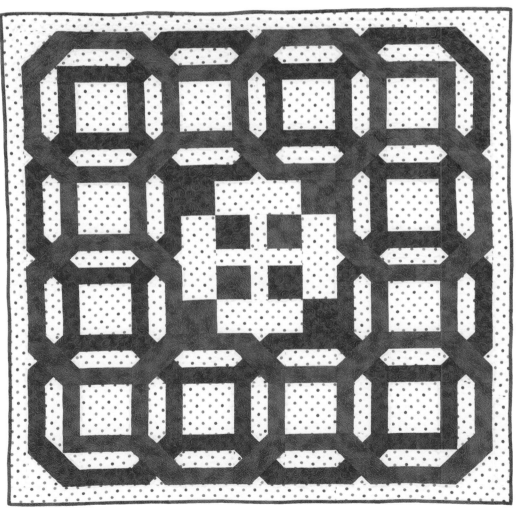

Waiting for Santa Stocking

Who says it has to be red and green to be Christmas?
Bright pink and lime green have now made their way to the mantel.
Sandy's daughter has already claimed this "girly" pieced stocking for her
college dorm room. As long as she doesn't expect it be full when she gets it,
we know where it will be hanging this Christmas!

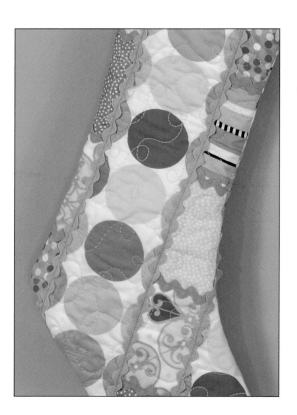

Skill Level: Beginner

Fabric & Stuff

Yardage is based on 42"-wide cotton fabric

- ½ yard large polka dot
- ¼ yard green stripe
- ¼ yard dark pink polka dot
- ⅛ yard each of four coordinating prints
- ¾ yard lining fabric
- 24" x 28" batting piece
- Thread to match fabrics and rickrack
- 7½ yards ½"-wide lime green rickrack

Cutting the Pieces

From the large polka dot, cut
Four 3½" x 21½" strips

From the dark pink polka dot, cut
One 2½" x 42" strip, then cut into
nine 2½" x 4" rectangles
One 3" x 8" strip for hanging loop

From each of the coordinating prints, cut
One 2½" x 42" strip, then cut into
nine 2½" x 4" rectangles of each fabric

From the batting, cut
Two 14" x 24" pieces

Making the Stocking

Prepare patterns for the stocking and cuff pieces, enlarging as directed on the patterns given on pages 54 and 55 and transferring the lines on the stocking pattern.

1. Sew six assorted 2½" x 4" pieces together on the short ends to make a strip. Press seams open. Repeat to make a total of six strips.

Make 6

2. Sew two 3½" x 21½" large polka-dot strips between three pieced strips to make a panel. Press seams open. Repeat to make two panels total. Stitch rickrack over all the seams of both panels.

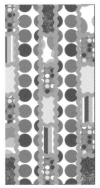

Make 2

3. Place one pieced panel right side up on a batting rectangle. Baste and quilt referring to Layering, Basting, and Quilting on page 93. Repeat with the second pieced panel.

4. Place the stocking pattern on one panel, aligning the vertical lines on the pattern with the seams of the large polka-dot strips. Trace around the pattern and cut out the stocking front. Reverse the pattern and place on the second panel. Cut out the stocking back.

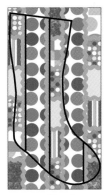 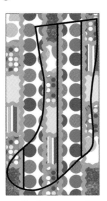

Front   **Back, reversed**

5. With right sides together, pin the stocking front to the stocking back. Stitch around the edges, leaving the top edge open. Press the seam open as much as possible. Turn right side out.

finishing the Stocking

1. Trace and cut two cuff pieces. Flip the pattern over to trace and cut two reversed cuff pieces.

2. Stitch a cuff piece to a reversed cuff piece on both short ends. Press seams open. Repeat with the remaining cuff pieces.

3. Position the two cuffs with right sides together and stitch along the pointed edge. Trim the cuff points and clip inside points into Vs. Turn right side out. Press.

Clip **Trim**

4. Pin the cuff in place over the end of the stocking, matching side seams. Baste in place ⅛" from the top edge.

5. Fold the 3" x 8" dark pink polka-dot strip in half lengthwise and press. Unfold. Fold each long edge in to meet the center crease. Press. Fold the strip in half along the center crease. Press. Stitch along the long edges to make the loop strip.

6. Fold the strip to make a loop. Baste in place over the side seam on the top of the stocking on the side opposite the toe.

7. Using the stocking pattern, cut a lining piece and a reversed lining piece, referring to step 4.

8. Pin and stitch lining pieces with right sides together. Stitch around the edge, leaving the top edge open and a 4" opening on the bottom edge. Press the seam open as much as possible.

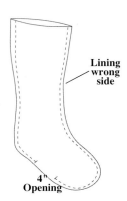

Lining wrong side

4" Opening

Outer shell
inside lining

9. Slide the lining over the stocking with right sides together. Stitch ¼" from the top edge.

10. Pull the stocking shell through the opening in the bottom of the lining. Stitch the opening closed. Push the lining into the stocking and pull up the hanging loop.

11. Stitch ¼" around the top edge of the stocking to finish.

Cuff Pattern
Enlarge by 250%

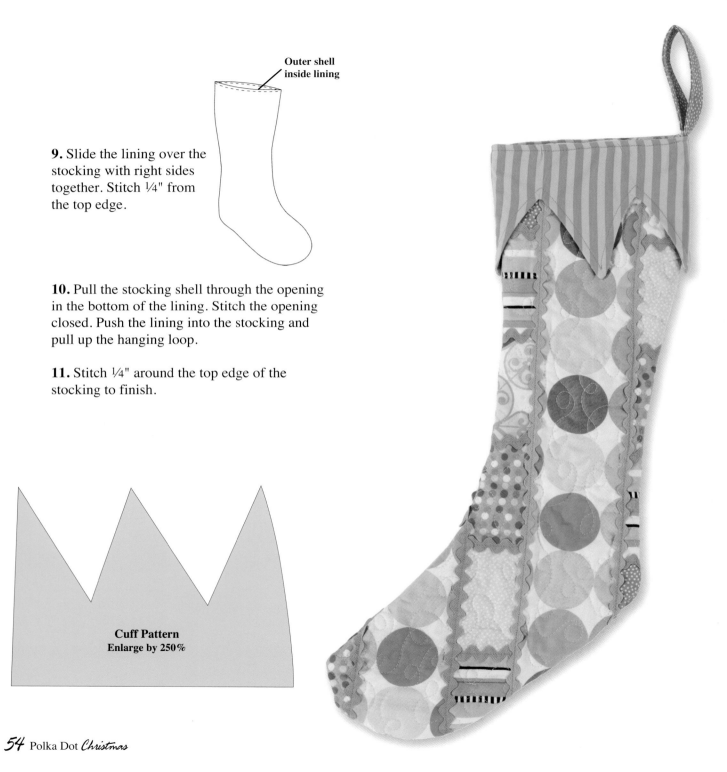

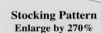

Stocking Pattern
Enlarge by 270%

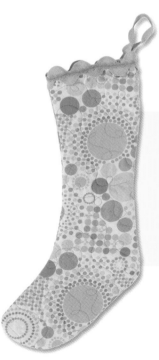

More Is Better!

Stitch up a bunch of stockings! Cut the front and
back pieces from a funky polka-dot print and add a
unique cuff. For the fur cuff, we used a 14½" piece
of 4"-wide fur trim, joined the ends and topstitched it
around the top of the completed stocking. For the
rickrack cuff, we cut 14½" pieces of jumbo and
medium rickrack, stitched them together, joined the
ends and stitched around the top of the stocking.

Pointsettia Hopscotch

Mix up poinsettias and big polka dots in an easy-to-piece design,
and you have all the makings of a cuddly holiday quilt.

Finished Size: 65" x 79"
Finished Block Size: 14" x 14"
Skill Level: Beginner

Fabric & Stuff

Yardage is based on 42"-wide cotton fabric

- 1⅔ yards light olive print
- 1⅔ yards poinsettia print
- 1⅓ yards red polka dot
- 1⅓ yards cream print
- 1⅛ yards dark green print
- ½ yard stripe
- 73" x 87" backing piece
- 73" x 87" batting piece
- Thread to match fabrics

Cutting the Pieces

From the light olive print, cut
  Twenty 1½" x 42" strips, then cut ten into
    forty 1½" x 10½" strips
  Seven 3½" x 42" strips

From the poinsettia print, cut
  Five 8½" x 42" strips
  Three 4½" x 42" strips, then cut into
    twenty 4½" x 4½" squares

From the red polka-dot print, cut
  Three 7½" x 42" strips
  Eight 2½" x 42" strips, then cut into
    twenty 2½" x 10½" strips and
    forty 2½" x 2½" squares

From the cream print, cut
  Three 7½" x 42" strips
  Eight 2½" x 42" strips, then cut into
    twenty 2½" x 10½" strips and
    forty 2½" x 2½" squares

From the dark green print, cut
  Seven 2" x 42" strips
  Eight 2½" x 42" strips for binding

From the stripe, cut
  Eight 1½" x 42" strips for binding insert

Making the Blocks

Note: Press all seams away from the block
center as each new strip is added.

1. Sew an 8½" x 42" poinsettia strip lengthwise
between two 1½" x 42" olive strips. Press seams
toward the poinsettia strip. Repeat to make a
total of five strip sets. Cut the strip sets into
twenty 8½" A segments.

8½"

A

Make 5 strip sets

2. Sew a 7½" x 42" red strip lengthwise to a
7½" x 42" cream strip. Press seam toward the red
strip. Repeat to make a total of three strip sets.
Cut the strip sets into forty 2½" B segments.

2½"

B

Make 3 strip sets

3. Sew a 1½" x 10½" olive strip to opposite
sides of each A segment to make 20 block
centers.

Make 20

4. Mark a diagonal line on the wrong side of each 2½" red square and each 2½" cream square. Place a red square on two corners of each block center and a cream square on the remaining two corners. Stitch on the marked lines, trim seam allowances to ¼", and press toward corners.

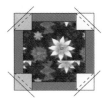

Make 20

5. Sew a 2½" x 10½" red strip to the red corner side of each block center and a 2½" x 10½" cream strip to the cream corner side. Sew a B segment to the top and bottom of each block center, matching red to the red side and cream to the cream side to complete twenty 14½" x 14½" blocks.

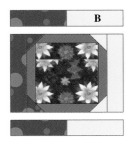

Make 20

6. Mark a diagonal line on the wrong side of each 4½" poinsettia square. Place a square on the cream corners of ten blocks. Stitch on the marked lines, trim seam allowances to ¼", and

press toward the corners to complete ten center blocks.

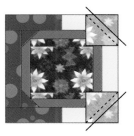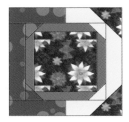

Make 10

Putting It Together

1. Join two blocks from step 5 and two center blocks from step 6 to make a row. Press seams in one direction

Make 5

2. Repeat to make five rows, alternating pressing direction from row to row. Join the rows to complete the 56½" x 70½" quilt center. Press seams in one direction.

3. Sew the 2" x 42" dark green strips together to make one long strip. Press. Cut two 70½" strips and two 59½" strips. Sew the longer strips to the sides of the quilt center and the shorter strips to the top and bottom. Press seams toward the strips.

4. Sew the 3½" x 42" olive print strips together to make one long strip. Cut two 73½" and two 65½" strips. Sew the longer strips to the sides and the shorter strips to the top and bottom. Press.

5. Referring to Layering, Basting, and Quilting on page 93, complete the quilt top.

Adding the Flat Binding Insert Finishing Edge

1. Sew the 1½" x 42" striped strips together to make one long strip. Press. Cut into two 79½" strips and two 65½" strips.

2. Referring to Flat Binding Insert on page 14, add the binding insert to the quilt.

3. Referring to Adding the Binding on page 93, use the 2½" x 42" dark green strips to bind the quilt.

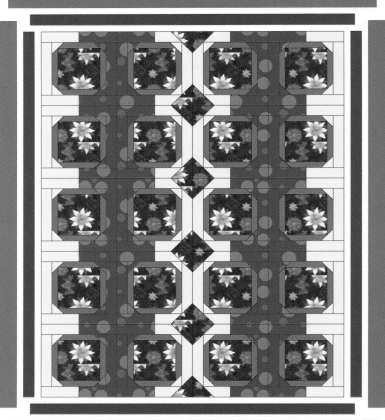

Quilt Layout

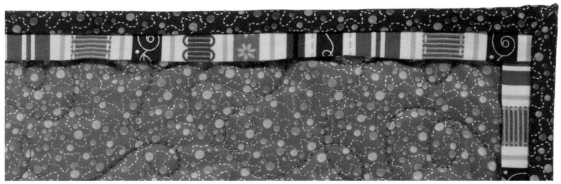

Flat Binding Insert Finishing Edge

Gift-It Tote

Think green for the holidays

(or any time of year) by stitching up gift totes, and stop using disposable gift bags. Make one for everyone on your list in fabrics and colors to match their personalities. But be careful, making these is addictive. Check out the different versions we made because we just couldn't stop.

Finished Sizes: 13" x 13" x 3"
Skill Level: Beginner

Square Tote
Fabric & Stuff

- ⅜ yard polka dot for the bag front and back
- ½ yard coordinating fabric 1 for the top, bottom, and sides
- ½ yard coordinating fabric 2 for handle
- ⅔ yard lining fabric
- 18" x 36" piece of fusible fleece
- Thread to match fabrics
- Four 25mm grommets
- Chalk pencil or other marking tool
- Two 2¾" x 12¾" pieces of heavy cardboard

Cutting the Pieces

From the polka dot, cut
Two 10½" x 13½" pieces

From the coordinating fabric 1, cut
Four 2" x 10½" strips
Two 3½" x 16½" strips
Two 2" x 16½" strips

From the coordinating fabric 2, cut
Four 3" x 42" strips

From the lining fabric, cut
Two 15" x 16½" lining pieces
Two 3½" x 13½" pieces

From the fusible fleece, cut
Two 15" x 16½" pieces

Making the Tote

1. Sew a 2" x 10 1/2" fabric 1 strip to the two short sides of a 10½" x 13½" polka-dot piece. Press seams toward the strips. Sew a 3½" x 16½" fabric 1 strip to the top and a 2" x 16½" fabric 1 strip to the bottom of each rectangle. Press seams toward the strips. Repeat to make two units total.

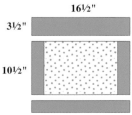

Make 2

2. Following the manufacturer's instructions, fuse the two fleece pieces to the back of the units from step 1. Quilt as desired.

3. Place the quilted sections right sides together. Stitch around three sides, leaving the top edge open.

4. At a bottom corner, align the side seam with the bottom seam to make a point. Stitch 1½" from the point to make a square corner. Trim off the point leaving a ¼" seam allowance. Repeat on the remaining bottom corner. Turn right side out to complete the tote shell.

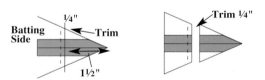

5. Place the lining pieces right sides together. Stitch around three sides, leaving the 16½" top edge open and leaving a 5" opening in the bottom edge.

6. Repeat step 4 to make square corners in the lining.

7. Place the tote shell inside the lining with right sides together. Stitch around the top edge.

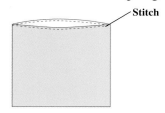

8. Turn right side out through the opening in the bottom of the lining. Smooth the lining inside the tote. Press the top edge. Stitch around the top ¼" from the edge.

9. Place the 3½" x 13½" lining strips right sides together and stitch around three sides, leaving a short end open. Turn right side out. Insert the two pieces of heavy cardboard inside. Fold the open ends in. Slipstitch end closed. Place in the bottom of the bag to make a sturdy base.

Adding the Handles

1. Make a mark 3" on each side of the center and 1½" from the top edge of the tote front and back.

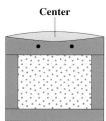

2. Position a grommet over each mark so that the mark is in the center of the opening. Trace a circle at each mark using the inside opening of the grommet. Cut out the marked circles. Insert a grommet in each circle following the manufacturer's instructions.

3. Place two 3" x 42" fabric 2 strips right sides together. Fold in half across the width, aligning ends. Cut ends at a 45-degree angle through all layers.

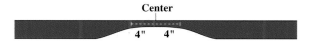

4. Stitch around all edges of the layered strips, leaving a 3" opening in the center of one side. Trim points and turn right sides out through the opening. Turn opening edges in ¼" and press.

5. Fold the strip in half along the length. Mark 4" on each side of the center as shown. Stitch close to the edge between the marks to close the turning opening and secure the folded handle.

6. Repeat steps 3 through 5 with the remaining 3" x 42" fabric 2 strips to make the second handle.

Looking for a more durable base for your *Gift-It Tote?* Use stiff plastic-canvas mesh instead of the heavy cardboard.

7. Referring to the photo, insert the ends of one handle strip through the grommets on the front of the tote, leaving about 8" above the top of the tote. Tie the ends in a square knot. Repeat with the remaining handle strip on the back of the tote to finish.

More Totes

Ornament Tote

To make the ornament appliqué for your tote, trace the polka-dot pattern on page 36. Fuse it to the front of the bag, add a bow at the top, and it's an ornament! For even more fun, try adding several polka dots to the bag for a collection of ornaments.

Crazy-Pieced Tote

Use your favorite method of crazy piecing to make two 13½" x 10½" front and back panels. Add a few special stitches and non-traditional fabrics to make a tote that is perfect all year long!

A Different Shape

Need a taller tote? It's simple. To create the taller shape, just make a few adjustments to the pieces and it's a new look. All you need to do is turn the front and back pieces to be 10½" wide and 13½" tall and cut the following pieces for the rest of the tote:

Two 3½" x 13½" top strips
Two 2" x 13½" bottom strips
Four 2" x 13½" side strips
Two 3½" x 10½" base strips
Four 3" x 42" handle strips

Oh! Christmas Tree Tote

To make the *Oh! Christmas Tree* version, refer to the instructions for the fusible-appliqué tree on page 28 and cut 5", 3", and 2" squares. Slice them somewhat diagonally and fuse them onto the front and back panels of the tote.

Merry Christmas Table Runner

Traditional looking Christmas prints in nontraditional Christmas colors — a fun combination. These are the fabrics we chose for this easy-to-do table runner. To add even more of a festive touch … polka-dot edges. We used the block from the *Polka-Dot Tree Skirt* with a few minor adjustments to show off the holiday fabrics.

Finished Size: 20" x 53", including polka-dot finishing edge
Finished Block Size: 12½" x 12½"
Skill Level: Intermediate

Fabric & Stuff

Yardage is based on 42"-wide cotton fabric

- 1 yard red check
- ½ yard light polka dot
- ½ yard holiday print
- ⅓ yard holiday floral
- ¼ yard green print
- 28" x 53" backing piece
- 28" x 53" batting piece
- 5" x 42" batting piece
- Thread to match fabrics

Cutting the Pieces

From the red check, cut
> One 3¾" x 42" strip, then cut into
> three 3¾" x 3¾" squares, cut twice
> diagonally to make twelve triangles
> Two 3⅜" x 42" strips, then cut into
> eighteen 3⅜" x 3⅜" squares, cut once
> diagonally to make thirty-six triangles
> Four 2¼" x 42" strips for binding
> Two 5" x 42" strips

From the light polka dot, cut
> One 7½" x 42" strip, then cut into
> twelve 2¼" x 7½" pieces
> Three 1¼" x 42" strips, then cut into
> two 1¼" x 38" strips and
> two 1¼" x 14½" strips

From the holiday print, cut
> Three 3½" x 42" strips, then cut into
> two 3½" x 39½" strips and
> two 3½" x 20½" strips

From the holiday floral, cut
> One 7½" x 42" strip, then cut into
> three 7½" x 7½" squares

From the green print, cut
> One 3⅜" x 42" strip, then cut into
> six 3⅜" x 3⅜" squares, cut once
> diagonally to make twelve triangles

Making the Blocks

1. Sew a green print triangle to a 3⅜" red check triangle. Press seam toward the red triangle. Sew a 3⅜" red check triangle to the green sides. Press seams toward the red triangles.. Sew a 2¼" x 7½" light polka-dot piece to the long side. Press seam toward the polka-dot piece. Repeat to make a total of twelve units.

Make 12

2. Sew a pieced unit from step 1 to opposite sides of each 7½" holiday floral square. Press seams toward the square.

3. Sew a 3¾" red check triangle to the ends of the light polka-dot piece in each of the remaining pieced units. Press seams toward the red triangles.

4. Sew a pieced unit from step 3 to the remaining sides of the holiday floral squares to complete three 13" x 13" blocks. Press seams toward the triangle units.

 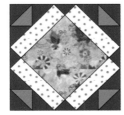

Make 3

Putting It Together

1. Referring to the layout below, join the three blocks to complete the 13" x 38" center. Press seams in one direction.

2. Sew the 1¼" x 38" light polka-dot strips to the long sides and the 1¼" x 14½" strips to the ends. Press seams toward the strips. Sew the 3½" x 39½" holiday print strips to the sides and the 3½" x 20½" strips to the ends of the runner center to complete the pieced top. Press.

3. Referring to Layering, Basting, and Quilting on page 93, complete the quilt. Using the four 2¼" x 42" red check strips, refer to Adding the Binding on page 93 to bind the edges.

Quilt Layout

Adding the Polka-Dot Finishing Edge

Using the polka-dot template on page 36, trace eight circles onto the wrong side of one of the 5" x 42" red check strips. Referring to Polka-Dot Finishing Edge on page 14, add four polka dots to each end of the table runner.

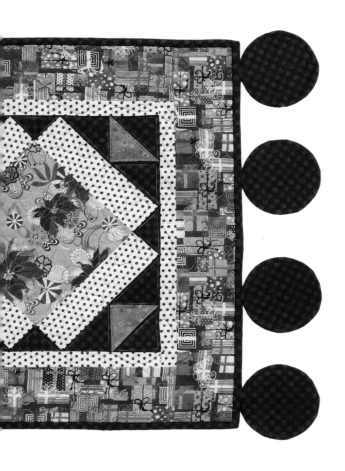

Wonky Northern Lights

We found ourselves using the word "wonky" a lot as we stitched this table runner. "Wonky rail fence squares" and "wonky prairie points" just seemed so fitting for the way these things tilted and turned and were anything but even. Hope you have as much fun making your wonky table-runner as we did!

Finished Size: 26" x 46", including prairie points
Finished Block Size: 5" x 5"
Skill Level: Beginner

Fabric & Stuff

Yardage is based on 42"-wide cotton fabric

- 1⅝ yards navy and white polka dot
- ⅞ yard light blue and white polka dot
- ⅜ yard gold print
- 30" x 50" backing piece
- 30" x 50" batting piece
- Thread to match fabrics
- 5½" acrylic square
- ½ yard fusible web
- Spray starch
- Template plastic or cardboard

Cutting the Pieces

From the navy and white polka-dot, cut
Four 3" x 42" strips
Two 2" x 42" strips
Four 2½" x 42" strips, then cut into
two 2½" x 38½" strips and
two 2½" x 22½" strips
Six 4" x 42" strips, then cut into
thirty-four 4" x 7" rectangles

From the light blue and white polka dot, cut
Four 3" x 42" strips
Two 2" x 42" strips
Three 1½" x 42" strips, then cut into
two 1½" x 35½" strips and
two 1½" x 17½" pieces

From the gold print, cut
Three 1" x 42" strips, then cut into
two 1" x 37½" strips and
two 1" x 18½" strips

Making the Rail Fence Blocks

1. Sew a 2" x 42" light blue and white polka-dot strip lengthwise between two 3" x 42" navy and white polka-dot strips to make strip set A. Press seams toward the navy strips. Repeat to make a second A strip set.

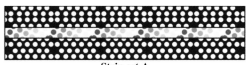

Strip set A
Make 2

2. Sew a 2" x 42" navy and white polka-dot strip between two 3" x 42" light blue and white polka-dot strips to make strip set B. Press seams toward the navy strip. Repeat to make a second B strip set.

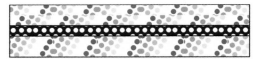

Strip set B
Make 2

3. Place the 5½" acrylic square at an angle at one end of an A strip set. Cut out the square using a rotary cutter. Repeat down the length of the strip set, butting the edge of each new square against the edge of the last one cut. Repeat with the second A strip set to cut a total of eleven of A blocks.

A Block
Cut 11

Tip

Give the strip sets a heavy coat of spray starch and press dry before cutting the A and B blocks. This will help to stabilize the bias edges of the blocks and prevent stretching.

4. Place the 5½" acrylic square angled in the opposite way on the B strip sets. Cut out ten B blocks.

**B Block
Cut 10**

Putting It Together

1. Sew a B block between two A blocks to make an A row. Press seams toward the A blocks. Repeat to make a total of four rows.

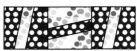

Make 4

2. Sew an A block between two B blocks to make a B row. Press seams toward the A blocks. Repeat to make a total of three rows.

Make 3

3. Sew the A and B rows together alternately to complete the 15½" x 35½" table runner center. Press seams in one direction.

4. Sew the 1½" x 35½" light blue and white polka-dot strips to the sides and the 1½" x 17½" strips to the ends. Press seams toward the strips.

5. Sew the 1" x 37½" gold print strips to the sides and the 1" x 18½" strips to the ends. Press.

6. Sew the 2½" x 38½" navy and white polka-dot strips to the sides and the 2½" x 22½" strips to the ends. Press.

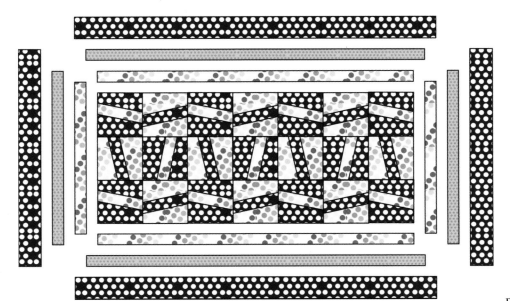

Quilt Layout

7. Using the star pattern on page 79, trace five star shapes onto the paper side of the fusible web. Following the manufacturer's instructions, fuse to the wrong side of the remaining gold print. Cut out stars on the marked lines and remove paper backing.

8. Referring to the photo below, arrange the stars on the center of the table runner. When you are pleased with the arrangement, fuse in place. Machine buttonhole stitch around each star using matching thread.

9. Referring to Layering, Basting, and Quilting on page 93, complete the table runner. Stop the quilting at least 1" from the outside edges of the table runner.

Adding the Prairie Points finishing Edge

The prairie points on this runner begin with rectangles. They are folded in a different way than is explained in the Prairie Points finishing Edge section on page 10. Refer to the following steps to make the prairie points and to the instructions on pages 11 and 12 to stitch them to your runner.

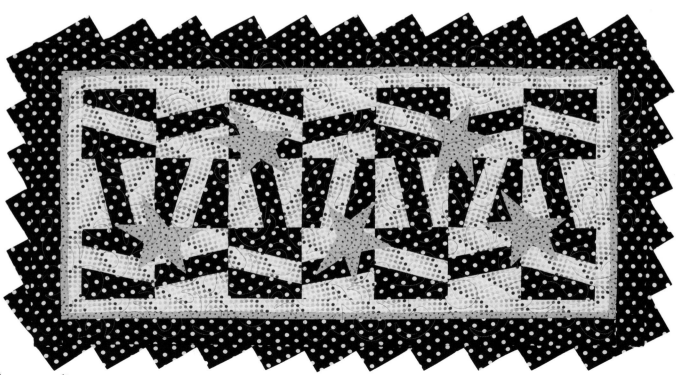

1. Fold the upper right corner of a 4" x 7" navy and white polka-dot rectangle down to the lower left corner. Press.

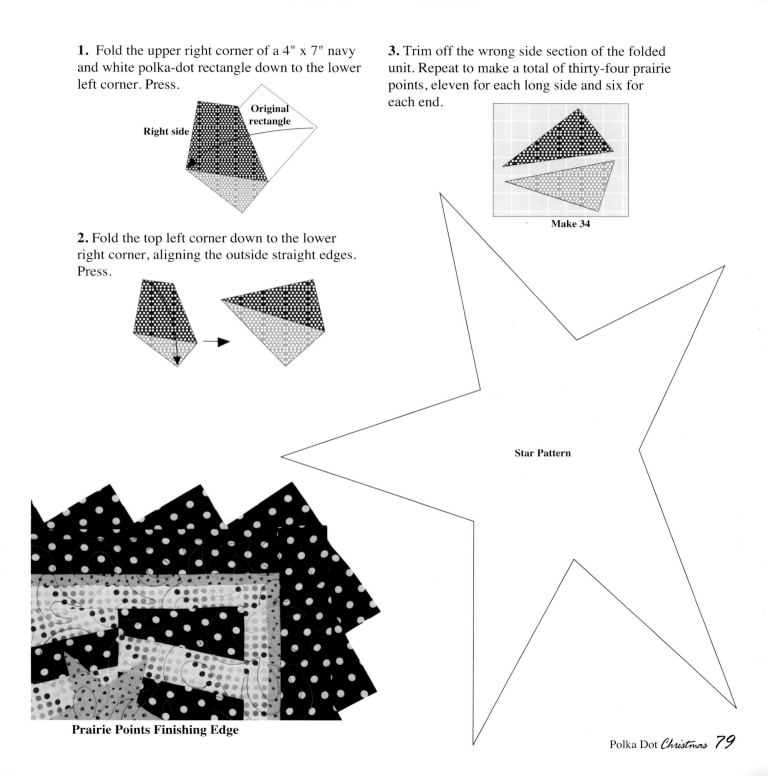

Right side

Original rectangle

2. Fold the top left corner down to the lower right corner, aligning the outside straight edges. Press.

3. Trim off the wrong side section of the folded unit. Repeat to make a total of thirty-four prairie points, eleven for each long side and six for each end.

Make 34

Star Pattern

Prairie Points Finishing Edge

Holiday Maze

When a single row of prairie points just isn't enough, add some more.
That's what we did with this table topper. The black points seemed okay,
but just not enough. We already had them stitched on and didn't
want to take out all those stitches. So we thought, "What if we just add
some smaller ones?" We did, and it made all the difference.

Finished Size: 46¼" x 46¼", including
prairie points
Finished Block Size: 9" x 9"
Skill Level: Intermediate

Fabric & Stuff

Yardage is based on 42"-wide cotton fabric

- 1 yard green print
- ⅞ yard cream polka dot
- ⅝ yard black print
- ⅝ yard black dot
- ½ yard red dot
- 55" x 55" backing square
- 55" x 55" batting square
- Thread to match fabrics

Cutting the Pieces

From the green print, cut
Four 2" x 42" strips
Four 2½" x 42" strips
Three 3" x 42" strips, then cut into
thirty-two 3" x 3" squares

From the cream polka dot, cut
Two 6⅞" x 42" strips, then cut into
nine 6⅞" x 6⅞" squares, cut once
diagonally to make eighteen triangles
One 3⅞" x 42" strip, then cut into
eight 3⅞" x 3⅞" squares, cut once
diagonally to make sixteen triangles
Four 2" x 42" strips

From the black print, cut
One 14" x 42" strip, then cut into
two 14" x 14" squares, cut twice
diagonally to make eight side triangles
and two 7¼" x 7¼" squares, cut once
diagonally to make four corner triangles
One 3½" x 42" strip, then cut into
eight 3½" x 3½" squares

From the black polka dot, cut
Four 4½" x 42" strips, then cut into
thirty-six 4½" x 4½" squares
Eight 3½" x 3½" squares

From the red dot, cut
Three 3⅞" x 42" strips, then cut into
twenty-six 3⅞" x 3⅞" squares,
cut once diagonally to make fifty-two
triangles

Making the Blocks

1. Sew a 2" x 42" cream polka-dot strip lengthwise to a 2" x 42" green strip. Press seam toward the green strip. Repeat to make a total of four strip sets. Cut the strip sets into seventy-eight 2" segments.

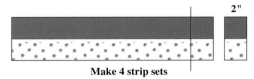

Make 4 strip sets

2. Join two segments to make a four-patch unit. Press. Repeat to make a total of thirty-nine units.

Make 39

3. Sew a red triangle to one side of twenty-six four-patch units. Press seam toward the triangle. Sew a red triangle to two opposite sides of the remaining four-patch units. Press seams toward the triangles.

Make 26   **Make 13**

4. Sew a two-triangle unit between two one-triangle units to make a center strip. Press seams away from the two-triangle unit. Repeat to make a total of 13 center units.

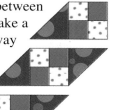

Make 13

5. Sew a large cream polka-dot triangle to the red sides of the center strip to complete one 9½" x 9½" Block 1. Press seams toward the triangles. Repeat to make a total of nine blocks.

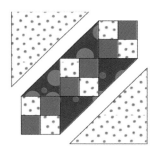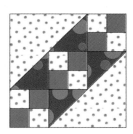

Block 1
Make 9

6. Sew a small cream polka-dot triangle to two sides of each 3½" black print square. Press seams toward the triangles.

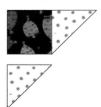

7. Sew a pieced triangle unit to the red sides of a center unit to complete one 9½" x 9½" Block 2. Press seams toward the triangles units. Repeat to make a total of four blocks.

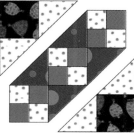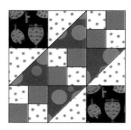

Block 2
Make 4

Putting It Together

1. Join the blocks and black print side and corner triangles to make five diagonal rows as shown. Press seams toward Block 2 and the black print triangles. Join the rows to complete the 38¾" x 38¾" center.

2. Sew the 2½" x 42" green strips together to make a long strip. Press. Cut two 38¾" strips and two 42¾" strips. Sew the shorter strips to opposite sides of the pieced center and the longer strips to the remaining sides. Press seams toward the strips.

3. Referring to Layering, Basting, and Quilting on page 93, complete the quilt top. Stop quilting approximately 1" from the outside edges of the quilt to add prairie points.

Quilt Layout

Adding the Prairie Points

1. Using the thirty-six 4½" black polka-dot squares for the large prairie points and the thirty-two 3" green squares for the small prairie points, refer to Prairie Points Finishing Edge on page 10 to complete the quilt. Begin prairie points ½" from each corner and use nine large prairie points and eight small prairie points on each side of the quilt.

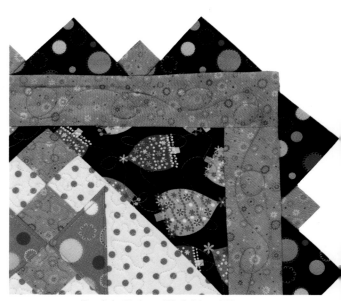

Prairie Points Finishing Edge

Ornament Wreath

We almost called this Recycled Table Topper because we used the scalloped border from the *Dots & Curves* quilt and the polka-dot ornament from the *Ornament Dance* quilt. It's an easy little project to stitch up in no time for a quick last-minute gift. It's also a great way to try a scalloped edge—not a huge commitment of time or fabric.

Finished Size: 31" x 31"
Skill Level: Beginner

Fabric & Stuff

Yardage is based on 42"-wide cotton fabric

- ⅞ yard red mottled
- ⅔ yard white tonal
- ⅝ yard blue holiday print
- Fat quarter each of three different polka-dot or stripe fabrics
- 39" x 39" backing square
- 39" x 39" batting piece
- ½ yard 18"-wide fusible web
- Thread to match fabrics
- 12" scallop template or template material
- Chalk pencil or another marking tool

Cutting the Pieces

From the red mottled, cut
Two 1½" x 42" strips, then cut into
four 1½" x 19½" strips and
four 1½" x 1½" squares
2½"-wide bias strips to total 192"
for binding

From the white tonal, cut
One 19½" x 19½" square

From the blue holiday print, cut
Two 5½" x 42" strips, then cut into
four 5½" x 19½" strips
One 6½" x 42" strip, then cut into
four 6½" x 6½" squares

Making the Wreath

1. Prepare a template for the polka-dot pattern given on page 36.

2. Cut four 5" x 15" strips of fusible web and fuse to the wrong side of each of the three assorted polka-dot and stripe fabrics and the red mottled.

3. Trace three polka dots on the paper side of each fabric. Cut out the polka dots on the marked lines and remove the paper backing.

4. Fold the 19½" x 19½" white square in quarters and crease to mark the center. Lightly mark a 10" circle in the center of the white square using a dinner plate or large bowl.

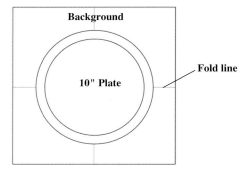

Background

10" Plate

Fold line

3. Arrange the 12 polka-dot appliqués around the marked circle, overlapping them in a pleasing arrangement. Fuse them in place to form the wreath.

4. Machine buttonhole stitch around each fused polka-dot to complete the wreath square.

Finishing the Quilt

1. Mark a diagonal line on the wrong side of the 1½" red squares. With right sides together, place a square on one corner of each 6½" x 6½" holiday print square. Stitch on the marked line, trim seam allowance to ¼", and press toward the corner. Repeat to make a total of four corner units.

Make 4

2. Sew a 1½" x 19½" red strip to a 5½" x 19½" holiday strip. Press seam toward the holiday strip. Repeat to make a total of four pieced border strips.

Make 4

3. Sew a pieced border strip to opposite sides of the wreath square. Press seams toward the strips.

4. Sew a corner unit to each end of the remaining pieced border strips, matching the red corners to the red strip. Press seams toward the strips. Sew to the remaining sides of the wreath square to complete the 31½" x 31½" quilt top. Press seams toward the strips.

5. Referring to Layering, Basting, and Quilting on page 93, complete the quilt.

The red of some of the polka dots shows through the white of the polka dots on top. We like the effect, but if it's not your cup of tea, fuse white medium-weight interfacing to the wrong side of the polka-dot and stripe fabrics before applying the fusible web.

Quilt Layout

Adding the Scalloped Finishing Edge

1. Fold the quilted top in quarters and mark the center of each side with a pin.

2. Prepare template for scallop pattern given on page 24. Place the scallop template at the center of one border strip. Mark around the curved edge. Repeat on each border strip.

3. Refer to the Scalloped Finishing Edge on page 8 to mark the corner scallops and complete the scalloped edge.

Scalloped Finishing Edge

finishing Basics

In this section we've included the finishing techniques that we use on our quilts.
Refer to this section for information as you create projects from this book.

Mitered Border

1. Cut and piece the border strips as directed in the project. Make a mark ¼" on each side of the quilt corners.

2. Center the border strips and stitch to each side of the quilt top, stopping and locking stitches at the ¼" mark at each corner.

3. Fold the quilt top in half diagonally with wrong sides together. Arrange two border strip ends right sides together.

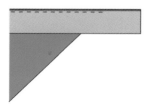

4. Mark a 45-degree angle line from the locked stitching on the border to the outside edge of the border.

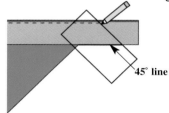

5. Stitch directly on the marked line, starting exactly at the locked stitch. Trim seam allowance to ¼".

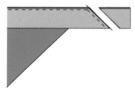

6. Press the mitered corner seam open and the seam between the border and the rest of the quilt toward the border.

7. Repeat these steps on each corner of the quilt.

Layering, Basting and Quilting

All the projects in this book were machine quilted by Sandy on her longarm quilting machine. You may choose to do your own quilting or take your projects to your machine quilter. Be sure that your batting and backing are at least 4" wider and 4" longer on each side of the project. The sizes you'll need are given in the Fabrics & Stuff section of each project.

If you would like to quilt your own project, there are many good books about hand and machine quilting. Check with your quilting friends or at your local quilt shop for their recommendations. Here are the basic steps to do your own quilting.

1. Mark the quilt top with a quilting design, if desired. Place the backing right side down on a flat surface and place the batting on top. Center the quilt top right side up on top of the batting. Smooth all the layers. Thread-baste, pin, or spray-baste the layers together to hold while quilting.

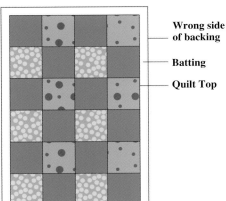

— Wrong side of backing

— Batting

— Quilt Top

2. Quilt the layers by hand or machine. When you are finished quilting, trim the batting and backing even with the quilted top. If you will be adding prairie points to the edges of your project, do not trim. Refer to Prairie Points Finishing Edge on page 10 for additional instructions.

Adding the Binding

The patterns in this book include plenty of fabric to cut either 2¼" or 2½" strips for straight-grain, double-fold binding. In some cases a wider binding or bias binding is needed because of a specific edge treatment. Extra yardage is included when necessary.

Preparing Straight-grain, Double-fold Binding

1. Cut strips as directed for the individual pattern. Remove selvage edges.

2. Place the ends of two binding strips right sides together at a right angle. Mark a line from the top left inside corner to the right bottom inside corner. Stitch on the marked line. Trim seam allowance to ¼".

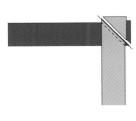

3. Join all binding strips into one long strip. Press seams to one side. Fold the strip in half lengthwise with wrong sides together and press.

Preparing Double-fold Bias Binding

1. Cut an 18" x 42" strip from the binding fabric. Place the 45-degree angle line of a rotary ruler on one edge of the strip. Trim off one corner of the strip.

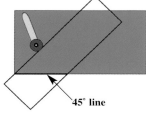

45° line

2. Cut binding strips in the width specified in the pattern from the angled end of the strip. Each strip will be approximately 25" long.

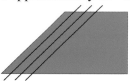

3. Cut strips to total the length needed for the pattern, repeating steps 1 and 2 as needed.

4. To join the bias strips, align the ends of two strips with right sides together. Stitch ¼" from the ends. Repeat to join all binding strips into one long strip. Press seams to one side. Fold the strip in half lengthwise with wrong sides together and press.

Sewing Binding to the Quilt

1. Leaving a 6"– 8" tail and beginning several inches from a corner, align the raw edges of the binding with the edge of the quilt. Stitch along the edge with a ¼" seam allowance, locking stitches at beginning.

2. Stop stitching ¼" from the first corner and lock stitching. Remove the quilt from your machine. Turn the quilt so the next edge is to your right. Fold the binding end up and then back down so the fold is aligned with the previous edge of the quilt and the binding is aligned with the edge to your right. Starting at the edge of the quilt, stitch the binding to the next corner.

3. Repeat steps to attach binding around the quilt, stopping stitching 6"– 8" from the starting point and locking stitches.

4. Unfold the two ends of the binding. Press flat. About halfway between the stitched ends, fold the beginning strip up at a right angle. Press. Fold the ending strip down at a right angle, with the folded edge butted against the fold of the beginning end. Press to crease folds.

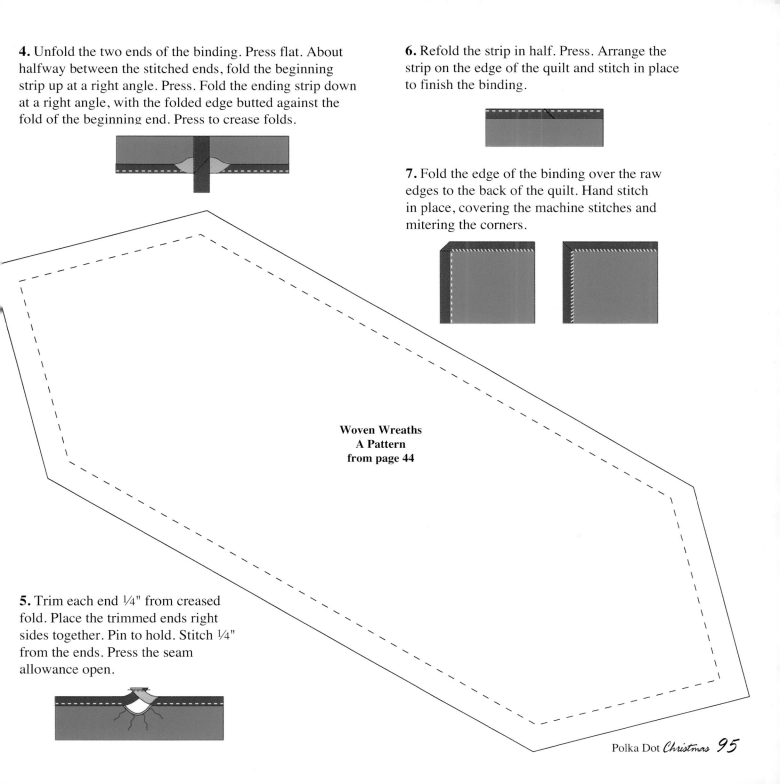

6. Refold the strip in half. Press. Arrange the strip on the edge of the quilt and stitch in place to finish the binding.

7. Fold the edge of the binding over the raw edges to the back of the quilt. Hand stitch in place, covering the machine stitches and mitering the corners.

Woven Wreaths
A Pattern
from page 44

5. Trim each end ¼" from creased fold. Place the trimmed ends right sides together. Pin to hold. Stitch ¼" from the ends. Press the seam allowance open.

About the Authors

Sue and Sandy have nearly 40 years of quilting experience between them. Sue began quilting in the mid-1980s after everyone in her family and all of her friends decided they didn't have another inch of space for anything cross-stitched. Sandy started in the early 1990s because she was so jealous of a quilt that a friend had made that she learned how to make one of her own. They have been working together on quilt designs for five years. They each also have their own quilting business.

Sandy is a longarm machine quilter. She bought her first machine in 1996 to finish her own quilts. She set it up in her bedroom, the only room big enough for the 12-foot table, and soon had quilters parading through the room picking up and dropping off their many quilt tops. She finally moved her machine and business from her bedroom to what was supposed to have been her husband's new garage. She jokes that there was never a vehicle in the building—the garage doors came out, walls went up and Sandy's Hideaway Quilts opened.

Sue began working for a national quilting magazine in 1995 as a technical reader and quilt designer. She assisted with development of a new quilting magazine and worked as one of its editors for many years. She continues to work as a freelance editor and technical reader for several publications. She has been busy designing and making quilts for publication during all of those years. She is the author of two books and coauthor of four others.

Sue and Sandy met in Sandy's bedroom! Sue's quilts needed to be quilted; Sandy was just the one to do it. In 2005, they decided to start collaborating on quilt designs, a fabric shop and kitting business. They formed Pine Tree Country Quilts, named because they each live in a grove of pine trees in the middle of Maine. They regularly design and make quilts for several magazines and fabric companies and put together fabric kits for their designs. They sell their kits and patterns to quilters around the world by phone and from their Web site, **www.pinetreecountryquilts.com.** This is their first book.